The John Roundtable

Debating Science, Strategy, and War

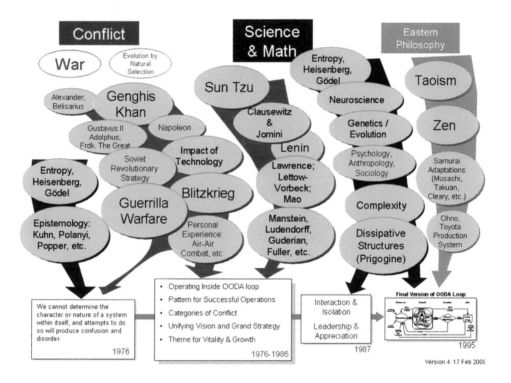

MARK SAFRANSKI (EDITOR) WITH DANIEL H. ABBOTT,
SHANE DEICHMAN, ADAM ELKUS, "LEXINGTON GREEN,"
FRANK HOFFMAN, DR. FRANS OSINGA,
DR. CHET RICHARDS, AND THOMAS WADE

NIMBLE BOOKS LLC

ISBN-13: 978-1-934840-46-7

ISBN-10: 1-934840-46-7

Version 1.0; last saved 2008-08-26.

Nimble Books LLC

1521 Martha Avenue

Ann Arbor, MI 48103-5333

http://www.nimblebooks.com

The cover font, heading fonts and the body text inside the book are in Constantia, designed by John Hudson for Microsoft.

Contents (including Figures)

FOREWORD

Thomas P.M. Barnett is Senior Managing Director of Enterra Solutions LLC, and author of Great Powers: America and the World After Bush *(February 2009). He blogs at* ThomasPMBarnett.com.

I've spent roughly two decades trying to move the military back closer to society, believing that the Cold War, during which military thought had become myopically fixated on nuclear strategy, had unduly isolated the military mind from messy, real-world applications and their associated dynamics, all of which had grown vastly more complex in the meantime. Not surprisingly, when the Cold War ended and our military peered unblinkingly into that teeming global landscape, it recoiled in the direction of familiar memes and sought desperately to fence off its responsibilities from that of the non-uniformed universe—i.e., the Powell Doctrine. But that effort proved fruitless and frustrating, both operationally and conceptually. Military officers found themselves delving deeply into the literature of business and technology, searching for Rosetta Stones that would reveal crosscutting connections.

The far harder row to hoe, however, was to re-examine military strategy itself to better contextualize it within the wider world. Until 9/11 arrived, this was a lonely and unappreciated pursuit—almost esoteric. But with that fateful day, and the complex wars/postwars spawned, such efforts took on new urgency. Translating some "new economy" management paradigm wouldn't be enough; we needed to rebuild our understanding of conflict from the bottom up, mapping out all relevant networks and their dynamics. Codification of that new understanding would come in the form of new/updated doctrine, a process that now proceeds apace—at least among the ground forces. But just as important would be the conceptual bridge-building to the non-military world, because, as each new doctrinal publication points out, what the military learns most in these recent operations is not what it must seek to control in terms of outcomes and effects, but that which it cannot possibly hope to control.

To truly think in grand strategic terms is hard because, in order to communicate concepts to the universe of relevant players, one needs a sort of "middleware" language able to traverse domains far and beyond the most obvious one of warfare. As America heads deeper into this age of globalization—a global order fundamentally of our creating—our need for such bridging lexicons skyrockets. In a networked age, everything connects to everything else, so most of what constitutes strategic thinking nowadays is really just the arbitraging of solid thinking regarding the dynamics of competition, leveraging the surplus of conceptual understanding in one realm to raise such understanding in others. That may sound like there's "nothing new under the sun," but more to the point, it admits that in today's still "unflat" world, the sun shines more brightly in certain locations and more dimly in others.

Today's military community must be able to speak in many tongues. It needs clear understanding of its own creeds and catechisms while simultaneously achieving a sort of operational non-denominationalism that will transform jointness into a serious "unity of effort" encompassing the rest of government, allies, host nations, and the private sector beyond. It needs, in short, a level of self-awareness never before achieved (e.g., this is what we do, how we do it, and *how it links up to everything else*), and a universal translator through which such descriptions can be transmitted to other communities.

This book of essays, based loosely upon an online roundtable discussion conducted by the authors concerning Frans Osinga's brilliant book, *Science, Strategy and War: The Strategic Theory of John Boyd,* builds upon Osinga's effort to explain and expand Boyd's efforts to create such strategic metalanguage, meaning a language that can be used to embed or contextualize strategic concepts among disparate domains. Boyd's legacy, as substantial as it is, survives only through such grammatical extensions, further pattern recognitions, and the like. Like any good gospel, his words are made living by means of social networks, so the fact that these essays emanated from bloggers engaged in online discussions is entirely appropriate to both Boyd's content and his ultimate aims.

INTRODUCTION

Despite having been an influential and controversial figure inside the Pentagon and defense policy circles, the late Colonel John Boyd has only recently come to wider public attention due to the excellent biography written by Robert Coram. Even so, much of what the public knows about Boyd relates to popular anecdotes of his connection to the F-15, F-16 and F-18 fighters, and Boyd's consultancy to then Secretary of Defense Dick Cheney on the eve of the First Gulf War. Of Boyd's ideas, the best known would be the OODA Loop (**O**bserve, **O**rient, **D**ecide, **A**ct) which has become a fairly widespread diagram in military literature and also in business management courses where competitive decision making is emphasized. Other than that, the corpus of Boyd's work is well known only to a relatively small number of his collaborators, reformers, theorists and military officers who were personally influenced by Colonel Boyd.

Figure 1. Colonel John R. Boyd (Estate of John R. Boyd).

This was partly Boyd's own fault. A tireless briefer and formidable mentor, Boyd wrote only a few formal papers and never attempted a magnum opus, preferring to evolve his thinking through the continual intellectual give-and-take of briefing sessions and an exhaustive schedule of deep reading, professional discussion and reflection. While Boyd's slides remain readily available at the websites *Defense and The National Interest* and *Chetrichards.com*, the situational context that Colonel Boyd created when he gave his talks is not always obvious to the viewer. As a result, an authoritative statement and analysis of Boyd's strategic theory had been lacking until now.

Science, Strategy and War: The Strategic Theory of John Boyd by Colonel Frans P. Osinga has filled that breach. A meticulous study of the origins and meaning of the ideas of John Boyd, Science Strategy and War has been endorsed as "The book John Boyd would have written" by no less than William Lind, a Boyd collaborator and the "Father of Fourth Generation Warfare." As such, *Science, Strategy and War* is the most complete exposition of Boyd's ideas that we are likely to see for some time to come.

But what are those ideas? Are they as valid and important a contribution to the art of war as Boyd's defenders and biographers claim? Do they have relevance in today's wars or offer wider application beyond military strategy? Had Dr. Osinga gotten to the heart of the matter in his book, *Science, Strategy and War* ?

These were the questions, among others, that an online roundtable in early 2008 attempted to answer. Hosted at *Chicago Boyz*, a popular libertarian and conservative group blog founded by Jonathan Glewirtz, the roundtable attracted the participation of an impressive group of reviewers from the blogosphere and from scientific, academic and military fields, including the author of *Science, Strategy and War,* Frans Osinga. This book is intended to be a reflection of that discussion of John Boyd's ideas but not a duplication or a verbatim transcript. There are significant differences.

This book contains sections of essays that were revised by roundtable participants, and differ from their original contributions, plus some supplementary material that was not previously posted. Some of the participants did not choose to have their essays reprinted here; also missing are the comments left by the audience at *Chicago Boyz* or at other numerous sites that linked to various posts. These can still be found by the interested reader, archived online at http://chicagoboyz.net .

Books and blogs are different media, each with their own virtues and intrinsic limitations, but they complement one another. The fast-paced, dynamism and freewheeling exchange of blog conversation versus the permanency and authority of the printed word. It has been the case that up until now that authors like Robert Scoble, Thomas P.M. Barnett, Nicholas Carr, Chris Anderson, John Robb, Frans Johannson and Don Tapscott have used personal or professional blogs to sell or enhance the narrative of their books and accumulate valuable feedback from their readers. We would like to suggest that the reverse holds true as well—that blogging at its best can generate insights and exchanges worthy of preservation by traditional publication as a book.

For that reason and in dedication to a man, Colonel John Boyd, who valued accomplishments over credit and those who strove to "do something" rather than to try to "be somebody", we offer up this book.

Mark Safranski, Editor

ABOUT THE AUTHORS

Daniel H. Abbott is a doctoral candidate at the University of Nebraska-Lincoln. He writes at the blogs _www.dreaming5gw.com_ and _www.tdaxp.com_. He has also written _Revolutionary Strategies in Early Christianity: The 4GW Against Rome and the COIN to Save It_, published by Nimble Books.

Shane Deichman is a nuclear physicist and the President/COO of EMC2 LLC. Deichman is the former Science Adviser to Marine Corps Forces-Pacific, was Experiment Operations Director at U.S. Joint Forces Command, and has served as director at scientific and private sector institutions such as The New England Complex Systems Institute, the Institute for Advanced Technologies in Global Resilience at Oak Ridge National Laboratory and at Enterra Solutions, LLC. He blogs at _Wizards of Oz_ and _Dreaming5GW_.

Adam Elkus is a freelance writer specializing in foreign policy and security. His work has appeared in _Small Wars Journal, Defense and the National Interest, The Huffington Post,_ and _Athena Intelligence._ He blogs at _Rethinking Security_ and _Dreaming 5GW_.

"Lexington Green" is an attorney and a blogger at _Chicago Boyz_.

Frank Hoffman, a former Marine Officer and national security consultant, is currently a Research Fellow at the Center for Emerging Threats and Opportunities at the Marine Corps Combat Development Command, Quantico, Virginia as well as at The Potomac Institute for Policy Studies; and a Senior Fellow at the Foreign Policy Research Institute's Center on Terrorism, Counter-Terrorism and Homeland Security. Hoffman is the author of _Decisive Force: The New American Way of War_ and a contributing author to the new U.S. Army/Marine Corps _Counterinsurgency Manual_.

Dr. Frans Osinga, the author of Science, Strategy and War:The Strategic Theory of John Boyd, is a colonel and fighter pilot in the Royal Netherlands Air Force. Osinga is also Associate Professor of War Studies at the Netherlands Defense Academy. Formerly, of NATO's Supreme Allied Command Transformation and Research Fellow, Clingendael Institute of International Relations.

Dr. Chet Richards is a mathematician and business consultant and was one of Colonel John Boyd's close associates and collaborators. The only authorized briefer of Boyd's *Patterns of Conflict,* Dr. Richards operates two websites dedicated to Boyd's strategic theories, *Defense & The National Interest* and *Chetrichards.com*. Dr. Richards is the author of numerous books on business and military strategy including *Certain to Win, A Swift Elusive Sword* and most recently, *If We Can Keep It*. Richards is also a retired Colonel in the USAF and was formerly the Reserve Air Attache in Saudi Arabia.

Mark Safranski is a teacher, educational consultant and an adviser to a privately held internet platform company, Conversationbase, LLC. Safranski blogs at *Zenpundit, Chicago Boyz, Complex Terrain Laboratory* and *Progressive Historians*. He is currently working on his next advanced degree.

Thomas Wade is a historian and a veteran of the war in Vietnam. He is an adjunct professor with Axia College, division of the University of Phoenix, online and teaches at Camp Pendleton, for Park Universities' military education program. Wade blogs at *HG's World*.

ACKNOWLEDGEMENTS

Behind the publication of any book, however modest in scope, stand many individuals who helped bring a concept to fruition. This book was no exception and it is a better book for their voices having been a part of it.

The idea of turning a blogospheric discussion of an intellectual biography of a military strategist, Colonel John Boyd, into a book was the brainchild of Nimble's publisher, W.F. Zimmerman. Fred Zimmerman has shown this first time editor inestimable patience. He was always at the ready with encouragement and direction when the process hit several "slow" periods. Without Fred's persistence, abetted by "Lexington Green" and Dan Abbott, there would very likely have been no book.

Colonel Frans Osinga, whose monumental *Science Strategy and War* was the catalyst for our discussion, was exceptionally generous with his time and contributions. Osinga is a "must read" for any scholar or military officer who seeks to get a grasp upon the evolution of John Boyd's strategic thought. I cannot recommend *Science, Strategy and War* highly enough for the serious student of military strategy and history.

Dr. Chet Richards, an experienced author and himself a foremost expert on the work of John Boyd, provided frequent suggestions and assistance during the editing process. His advice and insights were much appreciated and always to the good

Jonathan Gewirtz, the founder and site administrator of *Chicago Boyz* blog was the unobtrusive but invaluable host of the original roundtable discusson. Jonathan provided all the behind the scenes technical assistance for the contributors, moderation and promotion of the event. While he did not author a section Jonathan Gewirtz is as much a part of this book as any of the contributors.

Bill Nagl and Dave Dilegge, respectively the Publisher and Editor-in Chief of the always excellent *Small Wars Journal* are thanked for their permission and assistance in regards to the contribution of leading military analyst, Frank Hoffman, which first appeared in their *SWJ Blog*.

The heirs of the Boyd Estate are graciously thanked for their consent for the use of select photographs and materials from John Boyd's personal papers. Colonel Boyd's example, to borrow one of his phrases from *Destruction and Creation*, was the "dialectical engine" or motive force behind this book.

A HISTORY OF THE OODA LOOP

BY DANIEL H. ABBOTT

> *"To a certain extent the argument is valid that Boyd offered merely a synthesis of existing theories, a contemporary one, important and timely regarding the context of the 1970s and 1980s, but only a synthesis." Osinga, 2007, pg 29*

John Boyd's OODA Loop divides cognition into four processes, perception (called Observation), unconscious or implicit thought (called Orientation), conscious of explicit though (called Decision), and behavior (called Action). Frans Osinga's *Science, Strategy, and War: The Strategic Theory of John Boyd* does an excellent job describing the origins of Boyd's learning theory in the writings of Skinner, Piaget, and the cognitivists. However, Osinga's text excludes ongoing research into theories of learning related to OODA, as his text is focused on the development of the OODA model in particular rather than contemporary adaption. Fortunately, a recent review article by Jonathan St. B.T. Evans serves helps complete the picture, though the OODA loop is not mentioned there by name. Osinga's book is well worth purchasing, and can be thought of as prolegomena to all future OODA work.

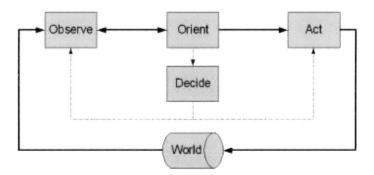

Figure 2. The OODA loop.

The "OODA loop," or "Boyd Cycle" (Osinga, page 2) is a dual-processing model of thought. That is, it supposes the existence of two separate central executives inside each human mind. This is supported by the recent psychological research, which also finds evidence for two different ways the brain exerts "will," differing in whether or not they regulate attention (Bargh, et al. 2001).The first of these, **Orientation,** is activated immediately by perception (called Observation by Boyd) and is capable of directly controlling behavior (likewise, called Action). Orientation is closely associated with long term memory. As Osinga writes on pages 236 to 237:

> *"In order to avoid predictability and ensuring adaptability to a variety of challenges, it is essential to have a repertoire of orientation patterns and the ability to select the correct one according to the situation at hand while denying the opponent the latter capability. Moreover, Boyd emphasizes the capability to validate the schemata before and during operations and the capability to devise and incorporate new ones, if one is to survive in a rapidly changing environment.... verifying existing beliefs and expectations, and if necessary modifying these in a timely matter, is crucial. The way to play the game of interaction and isolation is to spontaneously generate new mental images that match up with an unfolding work of uncertainty and change, Boyd asserted..."*

The second central executive, **Decision,** analogous to conscious thought, or what attention is spent on. As Osinga writes, "Decision is the component in which actors decide among actions alternatives that are generated in the orientation phase." Unlike orientation, decision faces limits in how much it can handle, and therefore relies on orientation to present it which simplified and categorized chunks in which to work.

John Boyd's model was purposefully designed as a cognitive and learning theory based on mainstream work within psychology. As Osinga writes on page 53:

> *"On 15 October 1972 he wrote from his base in Thailand to his wife that 'I may be on the trail of a theory of learning quite different and—it appears now more powerful than methods or theories currently in use'. Learning for him was synonymous for the process of creativity."*

In particular, Boyd's theory was based on the work of Jean Piaget, B.F Skinner, and the earlier cognitivists. Boyd combined each of these traditions, though revised some elements. From Piaget he both took the concept of mental structures, as well as suspicion of the power of logical analysis alone as a proper epistemological tool. To again quote Osinga (page 68):

> "Boyd also came across another source of uncertainty. As Jean Piaget asserted in the book Boyd read for his essay, 'In 1931 Kurt Gödel made a discovery which created a tremendous stir, because it undermined the then prevailing formalism, according to which mathematics was reducible to logic and logic could be exhaustively formalized. Gödel established definitely that the formalist program cannot be executed.'"

As Osinga describes in Chapter 3, "Science," Boyd drew from both Skinner and the cognitivists the power of environmental feedback. Consider the relatively trivial cognitive or cybernetic proposition on page 72 that:

> "A feedback loop is a circular arrangement of causally connected elements, in which an initial cause propagates around the links of the loop, so that each element has an effect on the next, until the last 'feeds back' into the first element of the cycle. The consequence is that the first link ('input') is affected by the last ('output'), which results in self-regulation for the entire system."

Osinga then proceeds to discuss the OODA loop as Boyd applied it, touching only briefly on Chapter 7 of some applications of Boydian thought to areas of military operations. However, Osinga does not emphasize the areas in which the OODA loop itself is still unique, but only compares it to either incorrect renditions of the OODA model (such as the "simplified" rendition Osinga shows on page 2) or to theories that preceded OODA (such as a cybernetic model without feedback and "(Reflex)" instead of orientation or System 2, on page 75).

Consider, for instance, two other models, one by Jon St. Evans published in 2006 and the other by Richard Moreno, published in 1990. Using different terms, the Evans model describes the role of Orientation (called by him System 1) and Decision (called by him System 2). Orientation or System 1 initially activates, and it may either lead to conceptual change or else inform further System 2 deliberation. However, Evans' model lacks the cybernetic or cognitive function of feedback, and does not describe how the last function would inform the first. Boyd's OODA loop, by attaching both Action and Observation to the environment, therefore may be described as a completed Evans model.

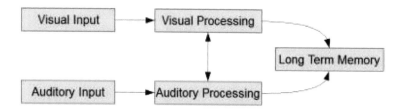

Figure 3. A simple model of information processing, adapted from Mayer (1996)

Likewise, the OODA loop completes the Moreno model. Moreno's description of learning focuses on the transformation of information in the external world to long term memory. In particular, Moreno's ongoing research focuses on the limited ability of explicit though to handle all information that should be learned. However, Moreno does not view long term memory as much other than an end-state for information (rather than the abode of Boyd's Orientation or Evans' System 1). Additionally, like Evans, Moreno does not connect the last stage of his model with his first.

Just as Osinga does not compare the OODA loop with other contemporary models, he does not describe contemporary research that further describes the difference between Orientation and Decision. The research on the subject is now well established. Evans' (2008) paper, "Dual-Processing Accounts of Reasoning, Judgment, and Social Cognition," provides a review of dual-proessing as it relates to how information travels through the mind. Klaczynski's chapter, "Cognitive and social cognitive development: Dual-processing research and theory," describes how the human dual-processing system boots up, from birth to adulthood. Countless more studies are coming out every month, and dual-processing studies, though they do not use the phrase, are all OODA studies and OODA science.

Frans Osinga's Science, Strategy, and War is a groundbreaking book on the OODA loop, describing in excellent detail how it originated. Buy it. What is needed now is a comparison of the OODA loop to contemporary theories of learning and an application of OODA in light of the newest research.

REFERENCES

Evans, J. St. B. (2006). The heuristic-analytic theory of reasoning: Extension and evaluation. *Psychonomic Bulletin & Review*, 13(3), 378-395.

Evans, J. St. B. (2008). Dual-processing accounts of reasoning, judgment and social cognition. *Annual Review of Psychology*, 59, 255-278.

Klaczynski, P. A. (in press). Cognitive and social cognitive development: Dual-process research and theory. J. B. St. T. Evans & K. Frankish (Eds.), *In two minds: Psychological and philosophical theories of dual processing.* Oxford, UK: Oxford University Press.

Mayer, R.E. (1996). Learners as information processors: Legacies and limitations of Educational Psychology's second metaphor. *Educational Psychologist*, 31(3/4), 151-161.

Osinga, F.P.B. (2007). *Science, Strategy, and War: The Strategic Theory of John Boyd.* New York: Routledge.

Bargh J.A., Gollwitzer P.M., Lee-Chai A., Barndollar K., Trotschel R. (2001) .The automated will: Nonconscious activation and pursuit of behavioral goals. *Journal of Personality and Social Psychology*, 81(6), 1014-27

THE ORIGINS OF JOHN BOYD'S *A DISCOURSE ON WINNING AND LOSING*

BY CHET RICHARDS

Boyd, like Clausewitz and Musashi, drew on the totality of knowledge in his day for ideas. As Frans Osinga, Grant Hammond, and Robert Coram all documented (and I know from personal experience), Boyd devoured his sources. We used to joke that if Boyd didn't write more in a book than the author did, it must not have been a very good book. As a result, he developed not just knowledge of, but fluency in most of these subjects.

Figure 3 shows the primary sources for the *Discourse on Winning and Losing*, which includes his 1975 paper, "Destruction and Creation," and his three briefings on strategy, *Patterns of Conflict* (1986), *Strategic Game of ? and ?* (1987) and *Organic Design for Command and Control* (1987). Boyd bound his last major briefing, *Conceptual Spiral* (1992), into later editions of the *Discourse* but this presentation, which explores novelty and the creation of knowledge, doesn't cite any new sources (it does present a long list of contributors to science and engineering on pages 9-12).

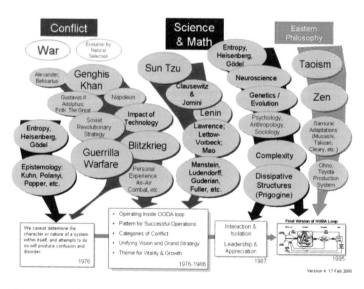

Figure 4. The origins of John Boyd's thought (Estate of John R. Boyd)

THE RED ZONE: MILITARY HISTORY AND STRATEGY

Sources in the red zone are largely documented within his works (the leftmost red zone is military history and the other is military strategy). People are sometimes surprised that Clausewitz had a strong influence on Boyd, but he did, particularly in the concepts of friction and centers of gravity. He accepted Clausewitz's definitions of these terms and refers to him throughout *Patterns* more than he does any strategist other than Sun Tzu, some 18 times on eight charts. Boyd's use of these ideas, though, often differed from how they appear in *On War*.

THE BLUE ZONE: PHILOSOPHY, MATHEMATICS, AND SCIENCE

The sources in the blue zone divide into two rough groups. Gödel, Heisenberg, the Second Law of Thermodynamics, and epistemology underlie "Destruction and Creation." The rest of the blue zone feeds into *Strategic Game*, *Organic Design*, and *Conceptual Spiral*. These sources are well documented in the texts themselves and in the "Sources" sections of "Destruction and Creation" and *Patterns of Conflict* (*Strategic Game* and *Organic Design* draw largely from these same sources). *Patterns*, however, makes little explicit use of philosophy, mathematics, and science. Of the other three, *Organic Design* relies most on what Osinga calls the "the new sciences," particularly complexity theory and the "dissipative structures" of physicist Ilya Prigogine, and proposes a concept of Orientation that can drive action either explicitly via the Decision box or, more often, implicitly through the "implicit guidance and control" link.

THE END OF (MILITARY) HISTORY

After *Organic Design*, Boyd turned away from military issues and his next briefing, *Conceptual Spiral*, is a philosophical exploration of the nature of novelty and the role of analyses and synthesis in generating it. It can be viewed as a return to the line of inquiry that he began with "Destruction and Creation" and offers a way of dealing with the "confusion and disorder" that paper describes.

Finally, in 1995, less than two years before his death, he produced a four-chart presentation with the audacious title, *The Essence of Winning and*

Losing. It distilled the conclusions from his previous work, but it is more than a summary. It includes Boyd's only depiction of the OODA loop and his only mention of "self-organization" and "emergence," two ideas closely associated with complexity theory.

Figure 5. Boyd in 1996. (Estate of John R. Boyd)

Why did he stop his investigation of military strategy? With the fall of the Soviet Union, the era of war deciding things among the major powers was over, and in his final years he investigated the roots of winning in any form of competition. This led him in two directions, the creative process as embodied in science and engineering in *Conceptual Spiral,* and business, most particularly the types of business strategy based around the Toyota Production System. The Toyota Production System (TPS) also struck him as an example of the novelty-generating process that he had examined in *Conceptual Spiral.*

We can't attribute his interest in the TPS to his personal affection for Toyotas—when I visited him in 1992, he had a Honda and a Mercury—but Taiichi Ohno's description of the Toyota System mirrored to an uncanny extent what Boyd had written in his earlier works on warfare. There's more on the parallels between *Patterns* and the TPS in my book, *Certain to Win.*

THE GREEN ZONE: TAOISM, ZEN, AND TOYOTA

Was this just a coincidence? It was not, as Boyd realized from Thomas Cleary's *The Japanese Art of War* (1991). Boyd was already familiar with the influence of Taoism on Sun Tzu and thence on Genghis Khan and Mao (and perhaps, from Genghis Khan, on the Blitzkrieg). Cleary's book, which became one of Boyd's favorites, linked Sun Tzu/Taoism through Zen to Musashi and the martial arts, which appealed to Boyd since his early career could be described as karate at 30,000 ft.

8

This stream also flows through Zen to present-day Japan and the Toyota Production System. Although he never included Zen explicitly in his briefings, we did discuss it when he was reviewing the early drafts of *Certain to Win*. I have no indication that Boyd ever practiced any Zen techniques.

The more research I do, though, the more striking the connections between Boyd's work and Zen concepts like clearness of vision, non-attachment to (fixed) forms and concepts, fluid awareness, and spontaneity. Although not mentioned in the text, Zen could have influenced the *Discourse* in at least two ways. First, as Osinga notes, it was part of his intellectual zeitgeist. Works on Eastern philosophy that Boyd is known to have read include:

- *Tao, The Watercourse Way,* Alan Watts
- *The Book,* Alan Watts
- *The Dancing Wu Li Masters,* Gary Zukav
- *The Book of Five Rings,* Miyamoto Musashi (several translations)
- *Sun Tzu's Art of War,* several translations
- *The Tao of Zen,* Ray Grigg
- *Zen and the Martial Arts,* Joe Hymans
- *Tao Te Ching,* Lao-tzu, trans. R. B. Blankney
- *Understanding Zen,* Benjamin Radcliff and Amy Radcliff
- *The Tao of Physics,* Fritjof Capra
- *Zen and the Art of Motorcycle Maintenance,* Robert M. Pirsig
- *The Japanese Art of War,* Thomas Cleary

And second, and this is my personal conclusion, his readings in Zen, particularly *The Japanese Art of War*, confirmed his emphasis on such concepts as implicit guidance and control, which appears in both *Patterns* and *Strategic Game*, and the overriding importance of Orientation, which he had designated as the *Schwerpunkt* of the OODA "loop" in *Organic Design*, chart 16. Combining these with Prigogine's ideas produced the OODA loop that appears in *The Essence of Winning and Losing*, a "loop" far removed from the cyclical version that he first employed.

IMPORTANCE OF UNDERSTANDING ORIGINS

What you're seeing here is the parts list for Boyd's snowmobile (see pages 6-9 of *Strategic Game*), his synthesis of the art of human conflict. It's sort of interesting, but not that important in and of itself. What is important is that you learn to build your own snowmobiles that will serve you in whatever situation you're in. As John concluded the *Discourse* (emphasis in original):

> *A loser is someone (individual or group) who cannot build snowmobiles when facing uncertainty and unpredictable change;*

whereas

> *A winner is someone (individual or group) who can build snowmobiles, and employ them in an appropriate fashion, when facing uncertainty and unpredictable change.*

When comparing Boyd to other strategists, it is important to place the others into historical context. A "color zone" chart for Clausewitz would be sparse by comparison—the red zones including personal experience and down through about Napoleon (excepting Sun Tzu), and the blue would stop at Newtonian mechanics. There would be no green zone at all. Such a comparison is, however, most unfair. Were Clausewitz to have lived in the late 20th Century, there is no reason, given his history, to think that he would have limited himself to the knowledge base of 1831 any more than Boyd did.

THE INTELLECTUAL LEGACY OF COLONEL JOHN BOYD

BY SHANE DEICHMAN

In an October 1939 radio broadcast, Winston Churchill described the Soviet Union as "... a riddle, wrapped in a mystery, inside an enigma." The same can be said of the late Colonel John Boyd, whose prowess as a fighter pilot and whose lectures on the relationship between energy and maneuverability revolutionized the U.S. Air Force—but who published no books. Rather, his legacy was left in a stack of acetate Vu-Graphs (thankfully, digitized by Chet Richards[1]) and reams of personal papers. For his studious review of the latter, distilling the mind of Boyd into book form, Col/Dr Frans P.B. Osinga deserves our gratitude. He has played Clausewitz to Boyd's Napoleon.

Figure 6. Boyd with an F-86.

In *Science, Strategy and War: The Strategic Theory of John Boyd*, Osinga presents us with a fascinating "deep dive" into the evolution of a brilliant thinker who devoted his life to applied learning and teaching. Though it is unfortunate that Boyd did not see fit to publish his theories in book form (unsurprising given his professional environment far from the Ivory Towers of academe), it is evident from his 1,500+ presentations that he rigorously developed and willingly shared his ideas. Boyd's stamina (both mental and physical) to lecture for more than a dozen hours at a time is testament to his devotion and his determination to succeed.

---

[1] http://d-n-i.net/second_level/boyd_military.htm

Osinga nicely complements the work of Boyd biographers (most notably Coram, Hammond and Richards) by dedicating the preponderance of his 300+ pages to how Boyd's thinking evolved—describing his intellectual influences from the expected (Sun Tzu, Clausewitz) to the unexpected (Popper, Kuhn, Polanyi). Particular attention is given to the influence of classical physicists (Newton) as well as quantum theorists and mathematicians (Heisenberg, Gödel).

Boyd embodied the now-popular notion of the "Medici Effect", a horizontal thinker who integrated perspectives across multiple, seemingly-divergent disciplines into a cohesive whole. His insights have proven applicable to a wide array of topics, and foretold of the emerging science of complexity theory (though I dislike Osinga's use of the composite term "chaoplexity", which undermines the distinction between "chaotic"—i.e., non-linear and seemingly random—and "complex"—i.e., a large number of interrelated properties or parameters). Given the swagger of the fighter pilot who bested the "best" in air-to-air combat in forty seconds or less, there is no doubt that Boyd—were he alive today—would be a prolific 'blogger, and a Chicago Boyz contributor whose inputs would outweigh all of our Roundtable writings combined.

While many associate Boyd solely with the "OODA Loop", he has given us far more than just a lexicon—just as contemporary grand strategist Thomas P.M. Barnett's work is far more than simply "Core–Gap" and "Leviathan–SysAdmin." Regardless of one's willingness to accept his ideas, the sheer effort Boyd invested in his research—and Osinga's effort in compiling the salient points for us—is an invaluable tool in anyone's intellectual toolbox.

The motto of the U.S. National Archives and Records Administration is *Litera Scripta Manet*: "The written word endures." It is ironic that intellectuals tend to revere the commentator more than the subject on whom they write: Herodotus over Leonidas, Thucydides over Pericles, Clausewitz over Napoleon. If history is consistent, then in a hundred years the name Osinga may be equally associated with the name of Boyd.

OSINGA'S JOHN BOYD THROUGH THE PRISM OF MILITARY HISTORY

BY THOMAS WADE

Col./Dr. Frans P.B. Osinga of the Netherlands Air Force wrote this work as his doctoral thesis. It is a superb, clearly written journey into the mind of a great thinker. For myself, someone who is seeped in the essence of history that for the most part took place before John Boyd's time, I found the book a stimulating read.

John Boyd, known as 40-second Boyd, for always being able to defeat an opponent in air combat within that time constraint, was a maverick, who left no great written treatise to explain his theories. What was left behind after his death were lecture notes and vu-graphs. Dr. Osinga carefully ginned those notes into a readable text and gave even the most un-military minded, a window on how not only John Boyd thought, but how humans and on a broader scale, all organisms adapt and survive.

John Boyd's legacy has been his OODA Loop (Observe, Orient, Decide, Action), some would conclude that his contribution is revolutionary, while others would conclude that it was based on selective cherry picking to support his thesis. The contributions of John Boyd are important because they draw from a vast store house of specialties, such as history, science, and behavior for support. He mulled these concepts over in his great mind and shared them in marathon lectures lasting up to 18 hrs.

The benefit of this work is to draw attention to Boyd's theory and stimulate thinking, something that in a modern technology centered universe, is often left to pre-conceived notions.

Boyd defined the Art of Success as:

> *Appear to be an unsolvable cryptogram while operating in a directed way to penetrate adversary vulnerabilities and weaknesses in order to isolate him from his allies, pull him apart, and collapse his will to resist; yet;*

Shape or influence events so that we not only magnify our spirit and strength but also influence potential adversaries as well as the uncommitted so that they are drawn toward our philosophy and are empathetic toward our success.

Boyd concludes with:

The first sentence is an advice to remain, in the words of Sun Tzu, unfathomable to the enemy, yet operate coherently in several levels of war and across different dimensions.

Multi-syllable words for a simple concept, survival.

Today, strategists debate what generation warfare we have now evolved too. I am no expert in those fields and would be treading on frozen cellophane to try and cross that river. This book helps us understand the changing environment of both war and peace. In a historical prospective, we can reach back into earliest time or to the remote jungles of New Guinea fifty years ago, when two men would meet in the forest, they would first, observe, then, orient to get best posture for survival, make a decision, kin or enemy, take action, fight or break bread. In the simplest terms, these decisions have played out in ever complicated scenarios ever since.

Dr. Osinga's book may turn out to be more read than any biography on John Boyd because he addresses the meat of what Boyd was trying to say in hundreds of lectures. He does this by providing the reader with Boyd's ideas to ponder:

Categories of conflict:

Three kinds of conflict

Based on his 'panorama' of military history, Boyd argues that one can imagine three kinds of human conflict:

Attrition Warfare—as practiced by the Emperor Napoleon, by all sides during the 19th Century and during World War I, by the Allies during World War II, and by present-day nuclear planners.

Maneuver Conflict—as practiced by the Mongols, General Bonaparte, Confederate General Stonewall Jackson, Union

14

General Ulysses S. Grant, Hitler's Generals (in particular Manstein, Guderian, Balck, Rommel) and the Americans under Generals Patton and MacArthur.

Moral Conflict—as practiced by the Mongols, most Guerrilla Leaders, avery few Counter-Guerrillas (such as Magsaysay) and certain others from Sun Tzu to the present.

In a historical sense, looking back to draw from the examples of strategies that worked or failed is most helpful when one realizes that an old saying frequently used by an old soldier I once knew, that the Army suffers from CRS—can't remember "scat"—is still the norm.

Compare Attrition Warfare with Maneuver Warfare.

- Spartans vs Thebans led by Epaminondas,who adopted the strategy at Leuctra. The strong left wing advanced while the weak right wing retreated.

- Or: Patton's end run around the Germans across France vs Hodge's attrition warfare in the Battle of Hürtgen Forest.

And Compare Moral Conflict with Attrition and Maneuver Warfare:

- Going to Vietnam ready to fight WW III, and finding ourselves fighting a stealthy foe, reminiscent of our own colonial Indian wars.

Dr. Osinga concludes that John Boyd's work serves a greater purpose than his OODA loop idea. Boyd's ideas involve much more than exclusively the idea of 'rapid OODA looping' or a theory for maneuver warfare. Contradicting those who categorically dismiss the validity of the OODA concept, the idea was found to be deep and rich in ideas, explanations, hypotheses, propositions, concepts and suggestions concerning conflict in general. These concepts are firmly based on a thorough study of military history and informed by insights on learning and the behavior of social systems derived from various disciplines.

What this book serves to tell us is that in order to survive, one has to be ready to adapt. This is illustrated in our current strategy in the so called Long War. The understanding of Boyd's strategy also relate in every aspect of life from the mundane to profound.

THE TWO COLONELS: OSINGA AND BOYD

BY MARK SAFRANSKI

Much of this roundtable discussion and the larger conversation on other sites, has centered on the merit of John Boyd's ideas and how well-deserved is his rising reputation as a strategic thinker. This is understandable, given the focus of *Science, Strategy and War*, it is natural to hone in on the subject of Dr. Osinga's study, the colorful and enigmatic Colonel John Boyd. I would like to take a moment and first consider the nature of *Science, Strategy and War* itself because this book represents a remarkably well-crafted example of scholarly writing.

With *Science, Strategy and War: The Strategic Theory of John Boyd*, which began as a doctoral dissertation, Colonel Frans Osinga engaged less in typical research and analysis than an expedition into intellectual archaeology. Boyd left a legacy that was at once impressive in terms of its depth and cognitive range, yet frustratingly elusive in the paucity and obscurity of the primary sources and the complexity and difficulty of the secondary ones. As many commentators have pointed out, John Boyd left behind no magnum opus; just a few formal papers, aging briefing slides, notes and copious marginalia furiously scrawled in books in fields as diverse as higher mathematics, classics, military history, theoretical physics, psychology, economics, philosophy, evolutionary biology and cybernetics.

The great historian Leopold von Ranke told his students that it was a historian's job to "...show how it really was." For Dr. Osinga, that meant getting into the head of John Boyd as his thinking evolved over several decades. For example, reading what Boyd read in order to ascertain how well Boyd understood, say, complexity theory or Clausewitz, postmodernism or Polanyi, Gödel or Guderian. Most scholars would find that kind of secondary reading—absolutely required before subjecting Boyd's briefs to a rigorous critical analysis—daunting. Thumb through the notes and bibliography of *Science, Strategy and War* and read the periodic commentary by Osinga on Boyd's use or exclusion of particular sources—for example, Schumpeter, Douhet, Liddell Hart and van Creveld. This is not an analysis that could have be done with drive-by citations and Osinga's effort shows in the resultant quality of *Science, Strategy and War*. Dr. Osinga, in my view, has "shown how it really was."

Osinga's John Boyd is a master synthesizer, itself a relatively rare intellectual quality, but also the author of highly original insights regarding the principles of moral conflict who wanted to teach his audience to be creative, adaptive, strategic thinkers who were hungry to survive and thrive in the competitive environment of life. Boyd was among the first to grasp that human organizations were really complex, adaptive, systems (what complexity theorist Yaneer Bar-Yam would call "superorganisms") that thrived or declined in accordance with Darwinian conceptions. Boyd was, as I infer from *Science, Strategy and War*, an apostle of dynamism and the ecology paradigm just now coming into vogue. It was a pity that Boyd died when he did as the subsequent advent of network theory and research into scale-free networks and modularity have done much to lend validity to his strategic speculations and reinforce his rejection of static, mechanistic, linear thinking in military affairs.

What remains to be done with Boyd or exists outside the scope of *Science, Strategy and War*? There is the matter of Boyd's influence on the 1991 Gulf War, acknowledged by senior officials but unknown in specific detail. Boyd's contribution to Marine Corps doctrine and other schools of thought (NCW, 4GW, EBO) have been dealt with piecemeal by other authors, notably Robert Coram, and Boyd's principal collaborators, but not in a systematic fashion. Boyd's efforts in the military reform movement also cry out for closer examination as well the continuation of the Boydian debate by Boyd's disciples and critics. These matters have yet to be brought under one roof in the manner that Frans Osinga has done with Boyd's strategic theory and remain as projects for investigation by future scholars.

Colonel Osinga has written a pivotal book in *Science, Strategy and War* that will be the touchstone text on John Boyd, an emergent classic at the intersection between 20th century intellectual history and strategic theory.

WHY DIDN'T BOYD WRITE A BOOK?

BY LEXINGTON GREEN

The study of the life and thought of John Boyd has taken a major step forward with the publication of Col. Osinga's *Science, Strategy and War: The Strategic Theory of John Boyd*. The earlier books are not superseded. Grant Hammond's *The Mind of War: John Boyd and American Security* is an overview, and probably the best introduction, with both biography and an overview of the ideas. Robert Coram's *Boyd: The Fighter Pilot Who Changed the Art of War* is more of a straight biography, focusing on the remarkable man more than the remarkable ideas. Where Coram drilled down on Boyd's life and personality, Osinga has drilled down on Boyd's intellectual foundations and his ideas. Osinga's book is the more challenging read, though it is written in a nicely plain and comprehensible style, given the rather dense set of ideas that Boyd formulated and conveyed. Osinga's book has a further strength. He is respectful but not worshipful of Col. Boyd. Rather than saying "Boyd was the greatest strategic thinker since Sun Tzu," Col. Osinga sets out what Boyd's strategic thought actually was, and lets the reader decide where he belongs (if at all) on the "top ten list."

I strongly suggest that anyone with the remotest interest in Boyd buy and read Col Osinga's book.

Col. Osinga's book suggests so many connections to other writers, to other issues, and to contemporary concerns, that I could have written a lengthy review essay just based on my many underlinings and marginal notes. Time and space will limit me instead to a few observations on one sub-topic.

Boyd presents an analytic and historiographic challenge. He was not an author. He did not write a book. He was nonetheless the originator and presenter of ideas and theories and arguments. He read a very large number of books, carefully, mining them for ideas, to fortify or challenge intuitions he had about conflict, strategy, winning and losing. Over time Boyd moved his reading more and more into realms paralleling his core interests, away from the realm of military history and theory, taking the idea of strategy to high levels of abstraction. Boyd looked for analogies, for insights which could only be gained standing outside the particular area of interest. In fact he believed that this process of "standing outside" was the only way to understand the system or subject under consideration.

Boyd organized his theories and arguments into briefings, not into books and articles, as an academic or journalist writer would be expected to do. The written residuum of these briefings is Boyd's slides. But the slides are only the skeleton of a briefing. Boyd himself gave life to the slides. Boyd's briefings were dynamic in all senses. Boyd was speaking and arguing, responding to the audience's questions, or even their expressions of irritation or agreement that may not have been voiced. The process was interactive, and as the briefings were given over and over, they were refined. Boyd's presentation slides evolved over time, and were subject to change at any time, though as he refined his presentations they firmed up. But, in theory, none of it was necessarily fixed.

Some of the contributors and commentators to this roundtable have offered the thought that it is "too bad" that Boyd never wrote a book. In a sense, Col. Osinga has provided the "bookification" of Boyd's final work, so if we want "Boyd's book," we now have the nearest approximation that is probably achievable. As Col. Osinga notes, there will be no more Boyd briefings. So, a compilation of what can be preserved is very much worth having.

However, the absence of a book from Boyd is not an oversight, nor is it to be regretted. Nothing Boyd ever said or did causes me to think he had any serious interest in writing a book. Time and energy are finite. The opportunity cost of writing a book, and all the attendant hassle, was not worth it to Boyd. He was doing something else.

Boyd had a famous speech he would make to people he encountered professionally whom he respected, which went, more or less like this:

> "... one day you will take a fork in the road, and you're going to have to make a decision about which direction you want to go. If you go that way you can be somebody. You will have to make compromises and you will have to turn your back on your

friends. But you will be a member of the club and you will get promoted and get good assignments. Or you can go that way and you can do something—something for your country and for your Air Force and for yourself. ...If you decide to do something, you may not get promoted and you may not get good assignments and you certainly will not be a favorite of your superiors. But you won't have to compromise yourself. To be somebody or to do something. In life there is often a roll call. That's when you have to make a decision. To be or to do? Which way will you go?"

I suspect that to Boyd, writing a book was more a "being" than "doing." Why? Surely writing a book, adding to the stock of ideas, setting those ideas out in the world in a coherent and permanent way is "doing"?

But what Boyd actually did—read, think, argue, and make live, in-person briefings—was more consistent with his own theories and his own ethic of "doing." This is true for several reasons.

First, Boyd was theoretically committed to "living, open-ended" systems. As Boyd put it:

> *"Gödel's Incompleteness Theorems, Heisenberg's Uncertainty Principle and the Second Law of Thermodynamics, all taken together, show that we cannot determine the character of a system within itself. Moreover, attempts to do so lead to confusion and disorder—mental as well as physical. Point: We need an external environment or outside world, to define ourselves and maintain organic integrity, otherwise we experience dissolution/disintegration—i.e., we come unglued.*
>
> *Living systems are open systems; closed systems are non-living systems. Point: If we don't communicate with the outside world—to gain information for knowledge and understanding as well as matter and energy for sustenance—we die out to become non-discerning and uninteresting parts of that world."*

By this analysis, once a book is written, it is dead. It is already superseded before the first copy is printed. Hence, Boyd kept his briefing process open. The Boyd briefing was a living and evolving thing in a way a putative "Boyd book" could never have been. Col. Osinga specifically notes Boyd's "deliberate refusal to 'finish' a briefing." The briefings were never set in stone, as a book would have to be. Again, this is not to say there is no value in writing and reading books. Boyd read lots of books. But he did not write one himself because he was doing something different from what book-writers do.

Second, a related point, Boyd may have realized that if he wrote a book it would have become a sort of "Koran." Once something is down in black and white, it takes on a life of its own. It becomes canonical, an Ur-text to be consulted for wisdom. Boyd was surely aware of his intensely charismatic style of leadership. He gathered a remarkable group of talented people as friends, students and allies. I suspect that he wanted to avoid, to the extent possible, a cult of personality, where his dynamic and living approach would harden into an orthodoxy. Some of this process seems to be happening in the writing of William Lind. For all the value of Lind's thinking and analysis, Lind has a "closed" and doctrinaire tone very much at odds with what I understand to be the Boydian approach. For example, Lind's enunciation of a small number of books as "the canon" is profoundly un-Boydian. Boyd's book-pile was ceiling-high, and he found analogies and metaphors and insights in books seemingly unrelated to military matters. There is not a fixed canon to understand strategy, nor can there be. Valuable books are where you find them, and they come along all the time, and the ocean of books is vast.

Just as the old German manuals had stamped on the examples provided "not a formula!", so Boyd's ideas cannot be applied in cookie-cutter fashion. Had Boyd written a book, the temptation to do this would be inevitable, since the "master" could be cited for this or that purpose, and legalist wrangling would replace analysis of real facts. As it is, the reduction of Boyd's thinking to "Boyd = (simple version) of OODA loop" is already unfortunately well advanced. Hopefully, Col. Osinga's book will help to arrest that trend.

Third, I will venture yet more speculation. Boyd's main aim, I think, was not the promotion of a set of ideas, or even an analytical approach, but the creation of a kind of person. This is the key thing he spent his time "doing." Boyd did of course believe in his OODA loop as a valuable and accurate insight. And he did of course believe that the kind of intellectual openness he taught was the correct way to study and think and approach problems. But he was not in the business of promoting "one killer slide". In fact, the OODA loop slide emerged late in the development of his thinking.

Boyd was aiming his presentations at his audience at multiple levels. At the lowest level, he could get the listeners to think in terms more akin to what he had discovered than they had previously done. Such listeners would be open to innovative ways of thinking and doing, at least. That was a minimum level of success.

A higher level of success would be to get his listeners to see that they needed to widen their thinking and step back from their preconceptions and look at a larger picture. This was particularly true in the Cold War era military. As the Cold War era ended and we began to face new and then inchoate challenges, Boyd was pushing his listeners to be open to radical rethinking. As Boyd put it:

> *"We can't just look at our present experiences or use the same mental recipes over and over again; we've got to look at other disciplines and activities and relate or connect them to what we know from our experience and the strategic world we live in."*

This is a demanding intellectual program for anyone who seriously tried to undertake it. Mastering the canonical material in one field is hard enough. Boyd is saying, be ready to go beyond all that, to look at what you do skeptically, from without, and be ready to use what you learn.

The ultimate level was demonstrated by his "elevator speech" to people who approached him and were drawn to his ideas: To create well-formed "doers."

> *The three levels then are (1) conveying ideas, (2) providing intellectual formation, creating a certain way of thinking, and (3) providing, beyond these, personal formation, creating people who operated to some degree as Boyd himself would have done.*

Boyd did not want to send forth from his briefings a bunch of people carrying a "how to" manual of Boyd's Greatest Hits. Rather, he wanted a large army of people who at least understood that there were alternative pathways to studying issues of professional concern, including the OODA loop, broadly understood. Beyond that, he wanted Boydian thinkers, who would at least take his analogic approach and look for patterns rather than formulas, etc. And beyond even that, he wanted, at the highest level, people who would adopt what we might term a "Boydian ethic".

Boyd's asceticism and intellectual drive, his sacrifice of virtually everything the world values for the development and application of his ideas, is a living embodiment of service. Of course, Boyd's life has the peculiarities of his particular and unique personality. But the larger message is—to do something great, to do something important, to live the warrior ethic of combat and sacrifice for victory, you will likely have to adopt the classical virtues of fortitude and humility and self-denial. Mere physical courage is not enough. People fear failure and humiliation more than death and wounds. Wars are often lost in a grey corridor somewhere years before the first shots are fired. Battles fought there, with no glory, no medals, no recognition, can be decisive. Boyd is asking: Can you be the person to fight those? Do you have what it takes, mentally and intellectually, but also in terms of personal character? So, to those who were open to it, Boyd was teaching not only with his briefing, but with his approach to life and service.

A book would have been a distraction from all that.

A FINAL NOTE

There is so much more in Col. Osinga's book that I wish I had time to discuss.

For example:

- There is an article to be written about the analogies between Boyd and Hayek, on the ideas of spontaneous order, and perpetually imperfect information.
- There is an article to be written about Boyd's concepts of cooperative behavior and Alan Macfarlane's study of the roots of civil society, i.e., theoretic v. empirical study of this phenomenon.

- There is an article to be written about the new scholarship on World War I and what Boyd might have made of it, and what it does to the growing orthodoxy of "4GW."

- There is a lot to be thought through and to be written about the idea that Boyd's seemingly more abstract thinking is in fact highly relevant. We now face a "Huntingtonian" world of cross-civilizational interaction and/or conflict between the USA (and/or the Anglosphere, and/or the "West") on one side, and the very different mental worlds of the the Chinese and Muslims on the other side. A "Boydian" cross-disciplinary approach is virtually mandated.

And I noticed these items only on a rather harried and rapid read-through of the book. A careful reading will suggest many other ideas for further analysis.

Col. Osinga has made a huge contribution by putting much of Boyd's thinking before us in a format which is orderly and usable. This achievement will make such further comparison and analysis possible in a way that they were not previously.

I look forward to a renaissance in "Boyd studies" inspired by this remarkable book.

APPLYING BOYD: IRAQ AND STRATEGY

BY ADAM ELKUS

How do the theories of John Boyd speak to America's most important international security issue, the war in Iraq? This is no idle question—if Boyd is as revolutionary a strategist as claimed, what do his ideas say about the war? Or rather, what does the war say about his ideas? I will examine Boyd's influence on network-centric warfare and the strategy of "shock and awe," as well as the Boydian subtext inherent in larger geostrategic issues.

"SHOCK AND AWE"

The operational phase of the campaign was heavily inspired by Boydian theory. US forces isolated, paralyzed, and destroyed Saddam Hussein's government in record-breaking speed. Many observers—especially retired military analysts on the major cable news networks—had predicted a quagmire. Despite my own (continuing) opposition to the war, it was surprising—and exhilarating—to see a murderous tyrant's apparatus of oppression rapidly smashed to bits with a minimum of American casualties.

The intellectual architect of the victory was Harlan Ullman, author of *Shock and Awe: Achieving Rapid Dominance*. Ullman's doctrine was heavily effects-based, using rapid and overwhelming force to attack the enemy's cognition. Every bombing, tank thrust, or combined arms attack was designed to sever the psychological, organizational, and technological bond that maintained the power of the Hussein regime. Although "Shock and Awe" is seen in the public eye as emblematic of the Bush administration's hubris, it was the perfect tool for destroying Baathist Iraq.

Authoritarian regimes are not known for their adaptability, and Iraq was no exception. Hussein denied his subordinates the autonomy to act on their own or report accurate information, keeping them in constant fear of purge. Worse yet, any politician or soldier that had managed to rise to the top of the Baathist heap did so because of patronage, not ability. There was no way such a paranoid, authoritarian, and brittle system could survive the violent shock that "Shock and Awe" put it through. One can compare the effect to that of the German blitzkrieg on Stalinist Russia in 1941.

Although the greater strategic literature of effects-based operations (EBOs) makes little reference to Boyd, it is not hard to see where the ideas originated. Boyd's *Patterns of Conflict* synthesized the airpower and maneuver warfare theorists and tied their strategies to ancient Eastern theorists such as Sun Tzu and Miyamoto Musashi. The end result was a strategy where force was designed to isolate, paralyze, and collapse the enemy instead of completely destroying his army. As Robert Corum and Grant Hammond recount in their biographies, Boyd's tireless briefings created the intellectual environment for the military to create Boydian-derived (and frequently overlapping) strategic concepts such as EBO, "Shock and Awe," and network-centric warfare (NCW).

Unfortunately, we quickly discovered that the terrorists and guerrillas that oppose us in Iraq have, as Ralph Peters put it, mastered network-centric warfare for "a tiny fraction of one cent on the dollar." Their networks have had tremendous success in targeting both Iraqi and American physical, mental, and moral centers of gravity with sophisticated military and psychological operations--a truly admirable 'effects-based operation.' Why is this?

A bipartisan chorus of critics has enumerated modern American military theory's failures against insurgents and terrorists. Theories such as network-centric warfare and effects-based operations are exclusively state-centric, they apply little to fighting insurgents, criminals, and terrorists, and they provide excuses for the Pentagon to sate the gluttony of defense contractors. Yet the real problem is that strategies like NCW, EBO, and "Shock and Awe" fail the most crucial Boydian test—they are all about destruction. They do not provide a means for, as Boyd would say, "vitality and growth."

As Rupert Smith recounts in *The Utility of Force,* the surest way to lose on today's battlefield is to focus solely on destroying the enemy. Every element of national power—military, economic, and political—is necessary for success. America has traditionally excelled at efficient, machine-tooled destruction. Traditional American military doctrine has not looked favorably

THE JOHN BOYD ROUNDTABLE

upon the kind of holistic political-military struggle necessary for counterinsurgency. Although the Bush's administration's epic failure in post-conflict planning has justly been savaged, there are many aspects of the wars in Iraq and Afghanistan that would be familiar to a Kennedy/Eisenhower-era Cold War hand like Edward Lansdale. We blunder about with little knowledge of the long-term consequences of our actions. From Iraq to the former Soviet state of Georgia, our short-sighted policies and strategies lack the kind of harmony and coherence that Boyd always stressed.

Our increasingly compartmentalized defense theories only multiply our confusion. Peruse any of the major military journals and you'll see a blizzard of differing strategies, strategic concepts, and position papers, all which seem to exist in isolation to each other. Perhaps Boyd's greatest strength was not the originality of his ideas, but his skill as a synthesizer, weaving the disparate strands of defense knowledge into a coherent worldview consistent from the tactical to grand strategic levels. Anyone familiar with American strategic history knows just how rare such synthesizers are.

The leading task for future generations of American strategists is to produce another grand vision for continued success and survival. Many have attempted this great challenge. Only time will tell which dreamer proves to be Boyd's intellectual heir.

MY STRUGGLE WITH BOYD

BY FRANS OSINGA

Boyd's work is titled *A Discourse on Winning and Losing* and the series of reviews and comments form exactly the sort of intellectual interaction Boyd sought to inspire. Judging by the quality of the reviews and comments it's been a very fruitful week that has propelled the Boyd debate into a wider arena and has, I hope, given it a renewed impetus. It has highlighted how we should approach Boyd's work as well as areas for further research.

Somewhat to my surprise there was only one seriously critical review that questioned Boyd's work, which was immediately hit upon in about 10 comments. I hope, and I believe Boyd actually would enjoy and encourage, that at some point we'll see a substantial effort which in Popperian fashion aims to critique either Boyd's work or my explanation/interpretation of his ideas, all in the spirit of the 'dialectic engine,' the term Boyd often used for describing his comprehensive OODA loop. The debate can use someone who can be to Boyd what Mearsheimer has been to Liddell Hart.

In fact, my own research on Boyd started out in that vein, but never got there. Instead of penning a 'rebuttal' to specific roundtable posts, perhaps I may absolve my obligation to conclude the roundtable discussion by adding some words concerning my own struggle with Boyd.

I first came across Boyd's name during the 1980s when, as a young cadet at the military academy, I (had to) read about this 'new' maneuver warfare school of thought. In the post Desert Storm doctrinal debates in NATO working groups I met Buster McCrabb, then at the faculty of the USAF School of Advanced Airpower Studies, who handed me a set of Boyd's slides (*Patterns of Conflict*). It did not make much sense to me and I could not quite see what the fuss was about. In 1998-1999 I was fortunate to study at the SAAS and attend an elective on Boyd by Grant Hammond who was then working on his Boyd biography. Armed with these lectures Boyd's slides began to gain meaning and depth, resulting in a chapter on Boyd as part of a larger paper in which I lined up a variety of strategists in the context of complexity theory.

Back in the Netherlands, as the Director of Strategy and Air Power Studies of the Netherlands Defence College, I started to expand this chapter with the aim to develop a critique, as I had the impression that the 'rapid OODA loop' idea was somewhat limited and that Grant's book was somewhat devoid of critical notes (which he admits by the way). It had already struck me that Boyd's personal papers hardly contained political science literature, nor did I see much in terms of air power and nuclear strategy. Moreover, I did not see all that much on decision making theory which I considered odd in light of my understanding of the OODA loop as a model of the decision making process. I therefore drafted a 60 pp. paper in which I lined up most major concepts concerning decision making such as Allison's models I-II-III, group think, Klein's RPD model, etc., and examined what others had to say concerning the influence of stress, experience and culture on decision making. In addition I looked for other cybernetic models en vogue in the past 3 decades in decision making theory, all this in order to assess the validity of the OODA loop model. Meanwhile, Grant Hammond came over to deliver several lectures on Boyd to my students. My research (and Grant commented gracefully on a whole series of immature drafts) and Hammond's lectures brought home to me three issues. First, after 150 pp of writing, I could not find that much fault with the comprehensive OODA loop and saw many similarities with other cybernetic models. Second, there was much more in Boyd's work than 'only' the rapid OODA loop idea. Thirdly, if I still intended to develop a well-founded critique, I first needed to explain Boyd because at that point there was no solid accepted academic interpretation of his work. This was during the summer of 2001.

By that time I was seconded to the Clingendael Institute of International Relations as the MoD Research Fellow. 9/11, Operation Enduring Freedom and Operation Iraqi Freedom for some reason required my attention and only during the summer of 2003 could I seriously pick up the Boyd research (which had been accepted as subject of my dissertation). By then I had discovered that any proper attempt to explain his work would require explaining his 'formative factors'. As any dissertation has distinct limits as far as length is concerned, it quickly transpired that explanation and not critique would be the main aim of my research (and the first 150 pp were therefore binned).

That brings me to the book. My discussion of his formative factors is somewhat imbalanced in the sense that it does perhaps not convey the depth of his study of military history, in comparison to his study of various scientific literatures (the Routledge edition is shorter on the science bit than the thesis by the way). I chose to highlight the latter because military history is actually the most common—and more straightforward—source that strategic theorists derive their arguments from. Moreover, the discussion of *Patterns of Conflict* would reveal Boyd's deep study of history and strategy anyway. Finally, I had the impression that Boyd gleaned quite a bit of original insights from in particular the scientific zeitgeist, but also that those insights came from studies not all that familiar to most people, and therefore in need of some elaborate explanation.

Initially I limited myself to those studies that were explicitly annotated and those that Boyd explicitly referred to (buying most of the books second hand at Powell's). It struck me how significant and deep the scientific developments have been during the years that Boyd developed his ideas and how many cross references one can find among the books Boyd read. I had problems with understanding information theory but secondary sources helped out with that. A fruitful visit to the archives at the USMC University at Quantico underpinned my suspicion that Boyd was 'deep' into science from the first moment on, and that in his subsequent explorations he continuously found confirmation of his initial impressions that he laid out in the essay *Destruction and Creation* and *A New Conception of Air to Air Combat*. It also highlighted that the influence of science grew over the years in comparison to military history.

In the end I had to hurry finalizing the thesis as I learned in September 2004 I was to be posted to HQ SACT, the NATO HQ in Norfolk, Virginia in January 2005. The thesis is therefore marred by a variety of editorial glitches. The subsequent Routledge edition has benefited from a major editorial (and painfully frustrating) process lasting about a year. It is shorter, more concise and it allowed me to add some relevant comments concerning Boyd's scientific sources. For both the thesis and the shorter book I want to acknowledge my considerable debts to Grant Hammond, Chet Richards, Barry Watts, Dick Safranski and Bill Lind.

My own view of Boyd (albeit biased)—briefly—is that he developed a very impressive, rich and coherent set of ideas, often with elements of profound novelty, with a wide range of applicability (see for instance the presentation of Chet Richard's et al on Boyd/4GW and the Iraqi insurgency, but also the various presentations/papers on the DNI site where Boyd's ideas are applied in an increasing number of environments). It is many things and refuses to be captured by one-liners or simple icons. In my presentation at the Boyd Conference last July I tried to convey a sense of 'what' Boyd's work is in the following slide.

A Discourse is:

> *An epistemological investigation*
>
> *A military history & search for patterns of winning and losing*
>
> *An argument against:*
>
> *- Attritionist mindset*
>
> *- Deterministic thinking & predictability*
>
> *- Techno-fetishism*
>
> *A rediscovery of the mental/moral dimensions of war*
>
> *A philosophy for command and control*
>
> *A redefinition of strategy*
>
> *A search for the essence of strategic interaction*
>
> *A plea for organizational learning and adaptability*
>
> *An argument on strategic thinking*

It must rank among the few general theories of war. He is certainly one of the prime contemporary strategists. Sure, his is not the final word on strategy. Indeed, he left an unfinished legacy, in line with his view that understanding war—a social behaviour with evolving features—requires a constant multidisciplinary search for improved and updated insights. Moreover, one will struggle if one wants to distil from Boyd's work distinct "how-to" guidelines for campaign planning. As with all major theorists and intellectual innovators there are also distinct "hooks" in his work for developing critique. But as a guide on what sort of intellectual attitude and

31

activity is required for understanding war and strategy I've found him invaluable. Trying to understand him was (and remains) a challenging but equally rewarding education. It has significantly broadened my intellectual horizon. Boyd made me think. And that was his whole point because *A Discourse on Winning and Losing* at heart is about "intellectual evolution and growth", as he wrote in the margins of a number of books.

As with Liddell Hart or Clausewitz, a period will come when his ideas will be dismissed, completed or improved upon. Areas for further research might be gleaned from my various shortfalls. I did not explore to the full the literature on business and management, as I could not find that many direct references to that literature in Boyd's work, nor have I properly assessed whether Boyd interpreted the various scientific literatures correctly. Although I believe Boyd was certainly not alone in applying concepts gleaned from the sciences to human behavior, perhaps he sometimes overstepped the bounds, but I have not explored that either. Neither have I examined fully to what extend Boyd was unduly selective or biased in his study of military history (although at times I've hinted at it).

Last week's roundtable itself however is indicative of the rising stature of Boyd, a decade after his death. This roundtable also confirms once more my view that, among the Western nations, the US harbors the liveliest intellectual environment for debating security and strategy related issues. From my perspective it was very gratifying—indeed flattering—to read all the positive comments. But I am also sincerely modest. The roundtable was first and foremost about Boyd's intellectual legacy, and I consider my book akin to the Sawyer or Cleary introductions to Sun Tzu; they serve as texts to tease out meaning of sometimes rather cryptic sentences and paragraphs handed to us by greater minds. As I've told Chet Richards, Dick Safranski, Grant Hammond, Bill Lind and Frank Hoffman, what pleased me most about their positive reviews of my book in the past two of years were their remarks that I've done justice to Boyd's intellectual efforts. That was my main aim but also my prime concern throughout the process.

Boyd generously shared his ideas, liberally handing out his presentations, all with the intent to educate. He would probably have loved the blogs .Let's spread the meme of Boyd's ideas.

UNLOCKING THE KEYS TO VICTORY

BY FRANK G. HOFFMAN

This article originally appeared in The Small Wars Journal Blog *and is published here with the author's permission.*

I first met John Boyd on a very warm summer day in 1983 at Headquarters, Marine Corps. Frankly he did not make much of an impression to a then young Captain of Marines. The briefer went through an extensive set of slides exploring conflict over the ages. I recognized the various strands of Clausewitz, Sun Tzu and Liddell Hart (and thus indirectly T.E. Lawrence) weaved throughout the pitch. In the aftermath of a long run and a too-large lunch, I preceded to take a somber tour of the insides of my eyelids.

This mental rest stop did not impress my boss, a Vietnam veteran who was taken with Boyd's ideas. As penance for my nap, he insisted I take the brief again the next day. Although I did not know it at the time, I never got a more valuable or more intellectually enriching experience over a decade in the Pentagon.

The intellectual contributions of the late Colonel John Boyd, USAF, have already been the subject of two fine biographies. Robert Coram's *Boyd: The Fighter Pilot Who Changed the Art of War* provided a window into Boyd's life as a fighter pilot, technical innovator and maverick defense reformer. Grant Hammond's *Mind at War John Boyd and American Security* summarized Boyd's main arguments. Both of these efforts are well regarded and helped rectify the limited record Boyd left behind. Regrettably, Boyd's career is too often truncated into well known "OODA Loop."

But Boyd had a lot more to offer. His contributions to flying tactics, fighter development, and operational theory are profound. The historical analyses and scientific theories he employed are not well documented nor well understood. This is principally due to Boyd's reliance on briefing slides. Colonel Frans Osinga fills out our collective understanding with *Science, Strategy and War*. In this very deliberate review, the author works his way through the arguments and source material of Boyd's famous briefs including *Patterns of Conflict* and *A Discourse on Winning and Losing*. He highlights the diverse sources that shaped Boyd's thinking and offers a comprehensive overview and remarkable synthesis of his work, and demonstrates that Boyd's is much more comprehensive, strategically richer and deeper than is generally thought.

Osinga is ironically a former F-16 pilot, a plane Boyd helped design, and a serving Royal Netherlands Air Force officer. He has lectured extensively in Europe, been posted at the Allied Command Transformation, Norfolk VA, and spoken at the annual Boyd Conference held in Quantico last July. The author is now stationed at the Royal Netherlands Defense Academy. This book, a version of his doctoral research, performs a superlative service as it expands our understanding of the utility of Boyd's work to modern conflict.

Over the years, my appreciation for John Boyd's intellectual achievement and moral character has grown. Others were less somnolent than I and quicker to understand what Boyd was offering. When he passed away in 1997, General Charles Krulak, then Commandant of the Marines, was quick to praise Boyd for his lifelong work in concepts, theory, and doctrine. General Krulak said that Boyd's theoretical contributions "rival those of the greatest military minds." Not only did he add considerably to America's understanding of the art of war, General Krulak credited him with contributing to the success of the U.S. military in Operation Desert Storm and as "one of the central architects in the reform of military thought which swept the services, and in particular the Marine Corps, in the 1980s."

The Marines attribute major influences in their fundamental doctrine of maneuver warfare to Boyd. He taught the Marines about competitive and intuitive decision making on the battlefield. He should be credited with stressing the importance of tempo as well as the time competitive nature of combat. Despite an Air Force background, he understood the proper role of technology in war. He is famous for insisting that "Machines don't fight wars. People do, and they use their minds." This emphasis on intellect and the human dimension found a home with the U.S. Marines, a Service with a valorous reputation but not previously open to intellectualism or doctrinal creativity. Boyd's stress on the psychological and moral dimensions of conflict over attrition-based strategies that emphasize firepower and technology resonated deeply with the Marines in the post-Vietnam era. Marine doctrine is infused with many of Boyd's critical observations, carefully transferred by Generals C. C. Krulak and Paul K. Van Riper.

In his concluding chapter, Osinga shows that Boyd's understanding of war is still very relevant. This important chapter underscores Boyd's grasp of the function of command and control, and the life of military organizations as a process of competitive discovery and interaction. This process of learning and adaptation was tied to Boyd's growing awareness of what we now know as complex adaptive systems. Colonel Osinga goes on to discuss the relevance of Boyd to the RMA debate, to Net-centric Warfare and to 4th GW. He correctly notes that Boyd would concur with the critical moral component of 4th GW but would have been leery about much of the RMA literature. He notes "it is unwarranted to see too much of Boyd's ghost at work here," since he would not have supported the emphasis on technology. However, "he certainly would agree with this emphasis on continuous innovation and agility."

Colonel Boyd's work remains relevant to the Small Wars community. His path finding work into organizational learning is the genesis for many follow on research efforts, including Lt. Col John Nagl's bestselling *Learning to Eat Soup with a Knife*. Boyd's emphasis on organizational fitness and constant adaptation in relation to a changing environment is the operational imperative in *FM 3-24 Counterinsurgency* (thanks to Dr. Nagl). Likewise, Boyd's exploration of what we now know as chaos and complexity theory was a decade ahead of its time. Students of the nonlinear sciences, including Dr. Dave Kilcullen, have exploited the concept of complex adaptive systems in relation to modern adversaries like Al Qaeda in his own ground breaking studies. Dr. Osinga makes it clear that we are still learning from the iconoclastic Boyd.

While John Boyd died in 1997, his influence lives on in the fighting doctrines of the Army and the Marine Corps, and in the halls of almost every educational institution of the U.S. military. This book explains why. *Science, Strategy and War* is a brilliant distillation of Boyd's research and the revolutionary theories about science and cognition he leveraged to better understand warfare. While the hardback price will scare off most readers, the new paperback version is more affordable and will make the book more accessible.

So while others have done more on bringing out the colorful life and the bureaucratic bashing personality of the irascible Boyd, no one has adequately framed his intellectual foundation in context, detailed his wide ranging research sources, or explored the full breadth of Boyd's undeniable intellect. Osinga's book is a long overdue corrective to those who too quickly dismissed Boyd's ideas as simplistic. *Science, Strategy and War* is a monumental contribution to military art and science, and is completely worthy of the genius it covers. This is an invaluable and prodigious piece of scholarship that belongs on the bookshelves of true professionals and anyone responsible for teaching strategy, operational art, and military theory.

John Boyd and Strategic Theory in the Postmodern Era

By Frans Osinga

This article originally appeared in Defense et Security Internationale *and is published here with the author's permission.*

The First Postmodern Strategist

We live in the postmodern era, the French sociologist Francois Lyotard told us in the early eighties. Postmodernism has come to signify a break with traditional modes of behavior. This includes warfare. Two dominant strands of strategic thought have both earned the label of postmodern warfare: Network Centric warfare (NCW) and Fourth Generation Warfare (4GW). One takes its inspiration from the postmodern information society, the other from the eroding authority and power of the modern-era political institutions. Both are also unified in a common conceptual father: the late USAF Colonel John Boyd, the first postmodern strategist[2]. Few people in the past three decades have surpassed his influence on western military thought, but, like Sun Tzu and Clausewitz, he has also often been superficially read and understood.

Boyd is most often associated exclusively with one key notion: the OODA loop, indeed the OODA loop picture has become iconic and has also become 'shorthand' for defining Boyd's work. The idea of the rapid OODA loop holds, in the popular interpretation that significant operational advantage will accrue to the side that can complete the decision cycle—Observation-

---

[2] For a full discussion of the postmodern aspects, chapter 7 of my book *Science Strategy and War, The Strategic Theory of John Boyd*, Routledge, Abingdon, 2007, from which this articles draws frequently, also for the various references to Boyd's work. This article also draws from "Boyd, Bin Laden and 4GW as String Theory," in John Olson (ed), *New Wars, New Theories; Prospects and Problems*, Oslo, 2008. This article allows for only a brief overview of some of Boyd's ideas, and not for critical remarks.

Orientation-Decision-Action—in the shortest time span. It asserts that information superiority is a decisive advantage, allowing for a greater tempo of operation. This suggests that disrupting the enemy's C2 process and improving one's own, is a key imperative for success. This notion of rapid-OODA looping, out-thinking the enemy, or getting inside his decision cycle, has become main-stream, and from Desert Storm to Iraqi Freedom US commanders such as Norman Schwarzkopf and Tommy Franks could be heard explaining their actions through these terms. This is an important idea and that concept alone suffices to demonstrate Boyd's continuing influence.

But this view is also too limited. The "rapid-OODA loop" idea too is too narrow an interpretation of the general OODA loop construct as Boyd employed it. His work *A Discourse on Winning and Losing* moreover harbors many other ideas beyond the OODA loop, including an argument on organizational culture. Boyd's work in fact constitutes a theory of strategic behavior in general, or in more precise terms, the dynamics of survival and growth of competing complex adaptive systems. A discussion of NCW and 4GW (although neither can be exclusively traced to Boyd's ideas) will serve not only to demonstrate the continuing influence of his work, but also to show what other arguments Boyd made beyond the OODA loop concept, ideas that continue to be of relevance today.

MANEUVER CONFLICT REFINED: NETWORK CENTRIC WARFARE:

Network centric warfare has been one of the fashionable buzzwords since the first article coining the term appeared in Congressional testimony in 1997. It lies at the heart of the Transformation program initiated by former US Defence Secretary Donald Rumsfeld, and since 2002 in only slightly different wording, the concept has entered NATO lexicon too as part of NATO Military Transformation.

NCW has a long lineage though and Boyd stands at the beginning of it. NCW is a direct extension of the maneuvrist approach to warfare, which was 'rediscovered' during the 1980s and early 1990s in the US military. Boyd's ideas and his advocacy were very influential in this process, which involved a change away from the attritional mindset. It found its articulation in the AirLand Battle doctrine and the revised US Marine Corps Doctrine, which regards war as a non-linear phenomenon, and harps on Boydian themes such as uncertainly, initiative, tempo, and adaptability, and agility. During the 1990s most western military doctrines started to display similar notions.

Three Boydian ideas in particular have found their place in NCW: (1) the idea of maneuver conflict; (2) the image of a swarm-like organization of netted but relatively autonomously operating units, acting in "synch" through an "auftragstaktik"[3]-based command and control set up and sophisticated information systems; and (3) the idea that information superiority will offer a decisive advantage because it allows a more rapid and accurate completion of the famous OODA loop, or decision cycle. Boyd's longest presentation *Patterns of Conflict* included an oft overlooked categorization of conflict models. The first model was the attritionist model, which Boyd rallied against. The second is the model of maneuver conflict. This holds that success comes not from firepower and destruction of the opponent but from the physical and mental dislocation of the enemy's units. What matters in planning actions is the expected cognitive impact of surprising, rapidly unfolding and varied physical lethal actions, and non-lethal threats and feints. One wants to create confusion, splinter the units, alienate the environment, inspire fear and uncertainty, and induce a lack of information so as to degrade trust, cohesion, and courage, and thus the ability to cohere and respond collectively, i.e., to adapt adequately as an organization. Affecting the ability to adapt in such a menacing and ever uncertain and dynamic environment, is one of Boyd's key themes, as is the focus on the cognitive features of the enemy's system.

Boyd's advice for organizational culture, structure and communication processes, is consistent with his emphasis on adaptability. The key challenge is maintaining cohesion while conducting fluid, varied and rapid actions, despite uncertainty and threats. In his presentation *Organic Design for Command and Control*, Boyd advocates an agile cellular organization - networked through ideology, shared ideas, experience, trust, goals and orientation patterns - that thrives in uncertainty and fosters innovation, creativity and initiative. Finding confirmation of his science-inspired ideas on

---

[3] "Mission-type tactics."

MARK SAFRANSKI ET AL.

adaptability and learning in historic works on command and morale and studies on individual and organizational learning, he considered trust and open communications between commander and troops vital, as well as a reliance on social bonds formed by implicit communications, training, shared experiences, doctrine, and clear objectives, combined with low level initiative and an tolerance for failure.

Whereas standard Pentagon solutions to uncertainty involved increasing investments in C4ISTAR equipment, Boyd aimed for creating adaptable and learning organizations consisting of informally networked teams that could comfortably operate in an insecure environment, due to their reduced information requirements. If everyone understands clearly, and is attuned to, the organization's purpose and/or the commander's intent, explicit communication beyond the objective is superfluous. Because of the shared outlook one knows what to do and what one can expect of others, be it supporting units, higher commands etc., implicit communication will suffice. Self-organization will be the result, a key NCW tenet.

In such an organization, command, Boyd indicates, is a wrong term, as is control. Boyd advocates lateral relations and continuous open two-way communication between hierarchies. Higher command levels must restrain themselves in their desire to know all that is going on at lower levels and to interfere. Higher commands must shape the "decision space" of subordinate commanders. They must trust and coach. They must encourage cooperation and consultation among lower levels. They must accept bad news and be open for suggestions, lower level initiatives and critique. It is thus more a question of leadership and appreciation of what is going on and comparing this to what is expected.

Such a set-up would enable rapid and varied actions in non-linear fashion—distributed operations is the term that is *en vogue* these days—all unified ("in harmony")—across the theater through a shared implicit perspective on the environment and an awareness of what is expected by higher commands due to the use of *Auftragstaktik*, and doctrine. While Clausewitz saw friction as an impediment, Boyd emphasized the creation of friction among the enemy units, and his proposed organizational set-up and mode of operations are geared to effectuate such a scheme.

In the literature of NCW we find these ideas applied to the military dimension of strategy[4]. NCW came about after a decade of discussions of the implications for warfare emanating from the changes in the economy, discerning a transition from the industrial age to the "Information Age." The transition to the Information Age implied, and was manifested in, the awareness that information was becoming the driving factor in warfare. Zooming in on particularly the information side of Boyd's OODA loop idea, many noted that information age technologies allowed for compressing the time to complete an OODA cycle. On the organizational and doctrinal level, these developments implied an empowerment of small units and the ability of armed forces to cover larger distances quicker, to influence events over larger swaths of territory, and to do more things in a given period of time. It offered a transition from attrition warfare to precision warfare or knowledge intensive warfare. With information the key weapon and target of the information age, the focus during a conflict must lie on disrupting, if not destroying information and communication systems on which the adversary relies in order to know itself: who it is, where it is, what it can do when, why it is fighting, which threats to counter first, etc. It means turning the balance of information and knowledge in one's favor.

The close parallels with Boydian military thinking also come to the fore in the consequences for organization and command and control philosophy. Arguing that the information revolution disrupts and erodes the hierarchies

---

[4] This discussion of NCW draws from Zalmay M. Khalizad and John P. White (eds), *Strategic Appraisal: The Changing Role of Information in Warfare*, Santa Monica: RAND, 1999; John Arquilla and David Ronfeldt, "Cyberwar is Coming," *Comparative Strategy*, Vol.12, No.2 (1993), 141-56; John Arquilla and David Ronfeldt, *Swarming and the Future of Conflict*, Santa Monica: RAND, 2000; DoD Report to Congress on NCW ,Washington D.C.: Department of Defense, CCRP publications, July 2001; David S. Alberts, John J. Gartska, and Frederick P. Stein, *Network Centric Warfare*, Washington, D.C.: U.S. Department of Defense, CCRP publications, 1999; David Metz, *Armed Conflict in the 21st Century: The Information Revolution and Post-Modern Warfare*, Carlisle Barracks, US Army Strategic Studies Institute, April 2000; and Chris Hables Gray, *Postmodern War, The New Politics of Conflict*, London, Routledge, 1997.

around which institutions are normally designed, several analysts predicted that adaptive organizations would evolve from traditional hierarchical forms to new, flexible, network-like models of organization. The information revolution would favor the growth of such networks by making it possible for diverse, dispersed actors to communicate, consult, coordinate, and operate together across greater distances, and on the basis of more and better information than ever before. Adopting a network structure is not an option but an imperative, for case studies strongly suggest that institutions can be defeated by networks and it may take networks to counter networks.

Several years later RAND analysts explored the idea that small units now had access to unprecedented levels of situational awareness, and could call in stand-off precision firepower offered new possibilities. They offered the "swarming concept" as the logical emerging paradigm in warfare, following three earlier paradigms in military history: the melee, massing, maneuver. The central idea is that information technology offers the potential for small networked units to operate as a swarm in a seemingly amorphous but deliberately structured, coordinated strategic way to strike from all direction, by means of a sustainable pulsing of force and/or fire, close in as well as form stand-off positions. It works best if it is designed mainly around the deployment of myriad, small, dispersed maneuver units that are tightly interconnected and capable to communicate and coordinate with each other at will and are expected to do so."

Introduced in the latter part of the nineties, NCW incorporated many of the concepts developed in various studies on the impact of the information age on warfare, including swarming and the network structure. With explicit reference to Boyd's OODA loop, NCW documents note that the advantage for forces that implement NCW lies in gaining and exploiting an information advantage. The network structure is essential, not a specific weapon or support system, the NCW Report to Congress states. NCW derives its power from the strong networking of a well-informed but geographically dispersed force. Such forces must have the capability to collect, share, access, and protect information, as well as the capability to collaborate in the information domain, which enables a force to improve its information position through processes of correlation, fusion, and analysis. This will allow a force to achieve information advantage over an adversary in the information domain. Importantly, in the "cognitive domain" the force must have the capability to develop and share high quality situational awareness and the capability to develop a shared knowledge of commander's intent. This will enable "the capability to self-synchronize its operations."

Boyd would likely not agree with the way technology has come to be such a dominant factor and with the expectations of some proponents that NCW would "lift the fog of war." On the other hand, he would agree with its organizational tenets and operational aspirations. In any event, it is not difficult to recognize key elements of Boyd's category of maneuver conflict and his preferred organizational characteristics.

MORAL CONFLICT REFINED: 4GW

The literature on 4GW emphasizes another dynamic but is equally deeply influenced by Boydian ideas, indeed, the first 4GW article published as early as 1989 was authored by one of Boyd's close associates, Bill Lind, and a group of like-minded officers[5]. While it shares the theme of adaptability and networked organizations with NCW, it is rooted more in guerrilla warfare theory and derives its inspiration from three additional ideas embedded in Boyd's work: (1) the image of war as a pendulum of action-reaction; (2) the concept of moral conflict; (3) the dynamic of interaction and isolation. In addition, it does not employ the narrow interpretation of the OODA loop but Boyd's own, more comprehensive rendition of it.

---

[5] This discussion of 4GW draws from William Lind, Keith Nightengale, John Schmitt, Joseph Sutton, Gary Wilson, "The Changing Face of War: Into the Fourth Generation," *Marine Corps Gazette*, Oct. 1989, 22-26; Greg Wilcox and Gary I. Wilson, "Military Response to Fourth Generation Warfare in Afghanistan," at http://www.emergency.com/2002/4gw5may02.htm, accessed April 9 2007; *The Sling and the Stone*, Zenith Press, St.Paul, Mn, 2004; William Lind, "Understanding Fourth Generation War," *Military Review*, September-October 2004; William Lind, Maj. John Schmitt and Col. Gary Wilson, "Fourth Generation Warfare: Another Look," *Marine Corps Gazette*, December 1991, 34-37; and Thomas Hammes, "War Evolves into the Fourth Generation," *Contemporary Security Policy*, Vol 26, Nr. 2, August 2005, 189-221.

In Boyd's own view, the OODA loop is much less a model of decision making than a model of individual and organizational learning and adaptation. In the words he used in the 1970s, it is a model of a "meta-paradigm," a "theory of intellectual evolution and growth." The first piece of *A Discourse on Winning and Losing* is an abstract investigation into cognitive processes, and the first key theme to emerge from this work is the fundamental uncertainty of our knowledge concerning our environment, with the subsequent need to continuously evolve our mental models so as to cope with the ever changing environment. We need to learn and adapt, and be comfortable with the idea that our view of reality is only partly correct, and only for a while. Each action or decision we take in that respect is just a test to see if our hypothesis concerning reality is correct. At heart the OODA loop is an epistemological model that is informed by the likes of Darwin, Heisenberg, Gödel, Popper, Bronowski, Kuhn, Polanyi, anthropologists such as Geertz, information theorists and cyberneticists such as Wiener and Neumann, system theorists such as Bertalanffy, and a host of others. French sociologists such as Lyotard, Derrida and Braudillard would feel quite comfortable with Boyd's postmodern view.

It follows that the abstract aim in any conflict is to render the enemy powerless by denying him the time to cope with the rapidly unfolding, and naturally uncertain, circumstances of war. The major overarching theme throughout Boyd's work is the capability to evolve, to adapt, to learn and deny such capability to the enemy. Boyd regards the contestants, the armies, their headquarters and societies in terms of living systems, as organisms, that aim to survive and prosper. To that end they—individuals, platoons, brigades, divisions, army corps, nations, and any other type of social system—observe, learn and adapt. The strategic aim, he asserts in *Patterns*, is "to diminish adversary's capacity to adapt while improving our capacity to adapt as an organic whole, so that our adversary cannot cope while we can cope with events/efforts as they unfold." At the most abstract level these efforts to survive and adapt resemble a game of "interaction and isolation": isolate an opponent and in due course it will lose internal cohesion and external support, its delayed and misinformed reactions will be ineffective and it will fail to adjust correctly to the changed environment. The aim is to change the opponent from an open into a closed system which slowly suffers the fate of all closed systems and the second law of thermodynamics, notions that found their place in his work: entropy. The corollary is the imperative to maintain constant interaction between the units of an organization and between the organization and its environment.

At the tactical and operational levels, adaptation can be seen as a function of speed of action and reaction and of information availability. At the strategic level, Boyd notes, adaptation is more indirect and takes longer time intervals. It revolves around adjusting doctrines and force structures and disorienting the opponent's orientation patterns, or mental images. At the grand-strategic level adaptability revolves around shaping the political and societal environment, including an attractive ideology, and adopting a mode of warfare the opponent is ill-suited to wage. Leaders should develop attractive and inspiring national goals and philosophies that unite and guide the nation as well as attract the uncommitted. Meanwhile they should demonstrate the ruling government is corrupt, morally bankrupt, disconnected from the population, and provoke enemy actions that are considered disproportional and ineffective.

Whereas NCW is geared toward the tactical and operational levels, and the conventional military realm, 4GW focusses more on these strategic and grand strategic levels of adaptation, on moral interaction and isolation and non-traditional modes of warfare. 4GW is part of a stream of publications that study non-western modes of warfare and asymmetric warfare, in which the political and moral aspects dominate over the tactical and technological. It is informed by Boyd's category of moral conflict: war is often played out in the moral dimension and is a contest of ideas and ideologies. Whereas NCW sees units bound by shared military relevant information, common tactics and procedures and doctrine, 4GW warriors are bound by shared ideology, values and worldviews. Their aim is to destroy the moral bonds that permit the adversary to exist. 4GW also follows as the next logical next step in the dialectic process that Boyd laid out in his overview of military history. His overview in *Patterns of Conflict* describes a continuous dialectic process of action-reaction, a constant interplay of offensive versus defensive measures, tactics, weapons and doctrines, and innovative responsive countermeasures.

Following this dialectic process, 4GW authors assert that warfare has evolved through four generations:

1GW: smoothbore weapons; line and column; conscription, rigid discipline with top down control. Example: wars of Napoleon.

2GW: rifled weapons, automatic weapons, indirect fire artillery; tactics still basically linear (esp. on defense), but firepower replaced manpower as predominant element; attempts to use "élan" to overcome firepower were now suicidal; nation-sate alignment of resources to warfare. Example: industrial age warfare such as the US civil war and WW I.

3GW: same weapons; but: non-linear tactics (infiltration/pull; surfaces & gaps); time rather than place as basis of operational art; emphasis on collapsing enemy rather than closing with and destroying him. Example: WW II, Blitzkrieg, armored and maneuver Warfare.

The next—fourth—generation comes not from promises that civilian technologies hold for the military (NCW for instance), but from contemporary societal phenomena that constitute more dominant influences on the nature of contemporary and future conflict, the reasons and motives they start or continue, the actors involved, the methods employed and parameters of success, for instance:

- The increasing vulnerability of modern open western societies and the loss of the nation-state's monopoly on violence .
- The low entry costs for waging 4GW in and against open societies .
- The eroding effect of globalization on the sovereignty of nation-states.
- The decline of the west, concurrent with the rise of Asia and the rise of the Islam.
- The rise of cultural, ethnic and religious conflict and the threat of radical Islam.
- The increasing irrelevance of old style hierarchies such as Western high tech armed forces.

Based on this view of trends, in 1989 4GW authors posed the hypothesis of Fourth Generation Warfare. First, the highly visible pattern of operations makes the West predictable and a deliberate response can be expected. They point out that precisely because the West has been highly successful in a certain style of warfare, other countries or groups will not abide by those rules. It goes beyond tactics and includes turning the Western conceptualization of war—its orientation pattern—against itself. The Western mode of thinking and waging war, which is founded on Clausewitzian principles, is giving rise to non-Clausewitzian styles of warfare. Instead of countering the West in the military dimension, nations but in particular non-governmental actors respond in the moral dimension. Arguing that the West has only ever been beaten in unconventional wars, practitioners of 4GW wage protracted asymmetric war. Regarding war not as a military but as a political struggle, they focus on the political will of western politicians and polities; exploit their impatience and casualty-sensitivity.

Second, the global societal developments push and enable this shift from high technology industrial age maneuvre war, focussed on the destruction of the enemy's armed forces to an information age focus on changing the minds of the enemy's political decision-makers through unconventional warfare. Small non-state entities increasingly gain options to generate destructive and disruptive power traditionally the privilege of nations. 4GW warriors combine guerrilla tactics or civil disobedience with the soft networks of social, cultural and economic ties, disinformation campaigns and innovative political activity to direct attack the enemy's political will. It is an evolved form of insurgency.

Politically 4GW involves transnational, national and subnational organizations and networks to convey a message to target audiences. Strategically it focusses on breaking the will of decision-makers. The message serves three purposes: to break the enemy's will; to maintain the will of its own people; and to ensure neutrals remain neutral or provide tacit support to the cause. Operationally it delivers those messages in a variety of ways from high-impact, high profile direct military actions to indirect economic attacks such as those designed to drive up the price of oil, or assassinations of specific government and company officials. Tactically, 4GW forces avoid direct confrontation if possible, while seeking maximum impact. They use materials present in the society under attack, be it industrial chemicals or fertilizers. This idea-driven fourth generation warfare will be a war fought at the ideological and moral level, with small highly maneuverable and agile cells employing standard guerrilla and terrorism tactics in a dispersed decentralized way, their actions informed, inspired, glued, and gaining coherence by shared programs, ideals and hatreds. 4GW opponents will deliberately not sign up to the Geneva conventions and use whatever means are available in a theater. There is a blurring of the distinction of peace and war and of the distinction between civilian and military. There will be no definable battlefields or fronts, instead the battlefield is highly dispersed and includes the whole of society. Terrorists use a free society's freedom and openness against it. Finally, 4GW warriors plan for long wars—decades rather than months or years. It is the antithesis of the high technology, short war the west favors.

4GW theorists find justification in a line of development that started with Mao's idea of The People's War, continued with Ho Chi Minh and Vo Nguyen Giap in Vietnam, and has reached a new stage with the Palestinian Intifada, which indicated 4GW warriors have now developed the ability to to take the political war to their distant enemy's homeland and destroy his will to continue the struggle. The dire warning is that many countries will evolve 4GW on their soil, in fact, 9/11 brought the changing nature into our living room, it is asserted. Most recent 4GW literature points at radical Islamist groups as the most immediate challenge, expanding outward as it does in every direction from its traditional heartland, including into Europe and the US. Other examples include Hezbollah's successes against Israel in the conflict during the summer of 2006; the murder of Theo van Gogh, the Dutch filmmaker; and the resurgence of the Taliban in Afghanistan, this time fighting NATO troops. Meanwhile Chet Richards, a key 4GW proponent and Boyd acolyte, has analyzed the 4GW insurgency in Iraq using Boyd's interaction-isolation dynamic and moral warfare model to show the strategic dilemmas facing US troops4[6].

---

[6] See Chet Richards, "Conflict in the years ahead," presentation, at http://d-n-i.net , accessed 10 October 2005.

4GW is not the end stage; 5GW is coming. The increasing use of easy to come by chemical toxic agents such as ricin or anthrax by "super-empowered individuals" or small groups is seen as symptomatic of it, which once more promises to make current western forces structures and defence policies irrelevant. This is "Open Source Warfare." As John Robb asserts in *Brave New War,* terrorism and guerrilla warfare are rapidly evolving to allow nonstate networks to challenge the structure and order of nation-states. It is a change on par with the rise of the Internet and China, and will dramatically change how we will view security. The same technology that has enabled globalization also allows terrorists, criminals and violent ideologues to join forces against larger adversaries with relative ease and to carry out small, inexpensive actions—like sabotaging an oil pipeline—that will generate a huge return. It is part of a trend in the process of putting ever more powerful technological tools and the knowledge of how to use them into an ever-increasing number of hands. The rise of malicious "smart mobs" is the downside of Friedman's flattening world. From Pakistan to Nigeria to Mexico it creates a new class of insurgents John Robb calls global guerrillas.[7] The new granular level, the realm of superempowered groups is where the seeds of epochal conflict now reside.

BOYD'S CONTINUING INFLUENCE

There are clearly many differences between 4GW and NCW, but the previous discussion also clearly highlighted that in their conceptual roots they share a common author. Both have many elements in common. Boyd actually made an effort in showing the underlying similarities in dynamics of maneuver and moral conflict. In his quest to fathom the dynamics of winning and losing, he stated that the essence is to[8]

- *penetrate an adversary to subvert, disrupt or seize those connections, centers, and activities that provide cohesion (e.g.,*

---

[7] See for instance John Robb's website, http://globalguerrillas.typepad.com/ globalguerrillas; this section draws in particular from John Robb, *Brave New World, The Next Stage of Terrorism And The End of Globalization,* John Wiley & Sons, New York, 2007.
[8] John Boyd, *Patterns of Conflict,* p. 98

psychological/moral bonds, communications, lines of communication, command and supply centers,...).

- *exploit ambiguity, deception, superior mobility and sudden violence to generate initial surprise and shock, again and again and again.*

- *roll-up/wipe-out, the isolated units or remnants created by subversion, surprise, shock, disruption and seizure.*

  These actions aim to: exploit subversion, surprise, shock, disruption and seizure to generate confusion, disorder, panic, etc, thereby shatter cohesion, paralyze effort and bring about adversary collapse.

For Boyd the message lies in the fact that in both concepts one operates in a directed yet more indistinct, more irregular and quicker manner than one's adversaries. This enables one 'to get inside their mind-time-space as a basis to penetrate the moral-mental-physical being of one's adversaries in order to pull them apart and bring about their collapse'. This discussion has demonstrated that Boyd's influence on contemporary strategic thought has been and continues to be significant, but also that for a full appreciation of that influence, one needs to go well beyond the narrow 'rapid-OODA loop' concept and fully engage with him in his *Discourse on Winning and Losing*.

A LETTER FROM THE PUBLISHER

Dear Reader,

As a military history aficionado, I first came across John Boyd's name in the early 1980's. I may have seen his name in a 1983 TIME magazine profile of Chuck Spinney, the defense reformer. Boyd's name stuck with me because I learned over the years that he was responsible for a pioneering general theory of air-to-air combat—"energy maneuverability"—and for a more wide-ranging collection of ideas that were influencing all the military services. However, as readers of this book know, Boyd did not leave a printed legacy, and it was hard to understand his work from what was readily available in print and online. Thus, it was with great interest that I came across the John Boyd Roundtable, and I immediately came to the conclusion that it would be a useful public service to publish a version of the Roundtable as a book.

The book-buying public has not yet spoken on whether this will be a successful experiment, but already this book is one of my favorite projects, for two fundamental reasons.

First, it adds something to the slender bundle of printed books devoted to one of the most important Western strategic thinkers of the 20th Century. That, in my view, is a service to both the United States and to Western civilization, as we are in the midst of a complex, painful, and ill-understood global struggle and transformation. As Thomas P.M. Barnett notes in his Foreword, Boyd's legacy, although substantial, is in the end only significant to the extent that it lives in the daily thoughts and activities of those who take it upon themselves to influence Western strategy in the 21st Century. I hope that this book helps make that happen. We need better strategy! And Boyd's approach, heavily influenced by history, science, and ethics, is consistent with the sort of world I want to see.

Second, each experiment in transforming good writing on the Web into printed form has special importance for Nimble Books—whose very mission, is of course, to be "nimble"—and for book publishing in general. Traditional book publishing is in the midst of its own great struggle and transformation, and for those of us who enjoy publishing the printed word, it is essential to experiment with new ways of doing things. I would not pretend that this experiment demonstrates a final, definitive, or flawless method, but there are a lot of good things happening between these covers.

I hope you agree, and if you are interested in sharing your thoughts on these subjects, please visit me at http://www.nimblebooks.com.

—Fred Zimmerman, Nimble Books LLC,
Ann Arbor, Michigan, USA, 2008

Printed in the United States
154580LV00003B